NATIVE AMERICAN NATIONS

THE SIOUX

BY BETTY MARCKS

CONSULTANT: TIM TOPPER, CHEYENNE RIVER SIOUX

BLASTOFF! DISCOVERY

BELLWETHER MEDIA • MINNEAPOLIS, MN

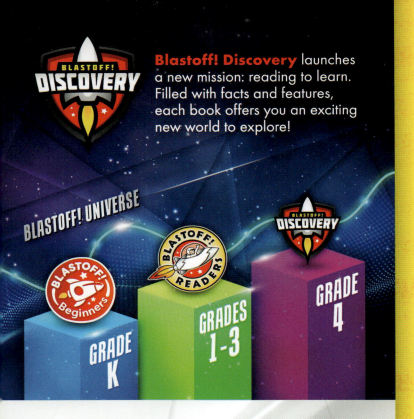

Author's Statement of Positionality:
I am a white woman of European descent. As such, I can claim no direct lived experience of being a Native American. In writing this book, however, I have tried to be an ally by relying on sources by Native American writers and authors whenever possible and have worked to let their voices guide its content.

This edition first published in 2024 by Bellwether Media, Inc.

No part of this publication may be reproduced in whole or in part without written permission of the publisher.
For information regarding permission, write to Bellwether Media, Inc.,
Attention: Permissions Department,
6012 Blue Circle Drive, Minnetonka, MN 55343.

Library of Congress Cataloging-in-Publication Data

LC record for The Sioux available at: https://lccn.loc.gov/2023028928

Text copyright © 2024 by Bellwether Media, Inc. BLASTOFF! DISCOVERY and associated logos are trademarks and/or registered trademarks of Bellwether Media, Inc.

Editor: Elizabeth Neuenfeldt   Series Designer: Andrea Schneider
Book Designer: Laura Sowers

Printed in the United States of America, North Mankato, MN.

TABLE OF CONTENTS

THE SEVEN COUNCIL FIRES	4
TRADITIONAL SIOUX LIFE	6
EUROPEAN CONTACT	12
LIFE TODAY	16
CONTINUING TRADITIONS	20
FIGHT TODAY, BRIGHT TOMORROW	24
TIMELINE	28
GLOSSARY	30
TO LEARN MORE	31
INDEX	32

THE SEVEN COUNCIL FIRES

The Sioux is a **confederacy** of nations who call themselves the *Oyate Oceti Sakowin*. This means "the People of the Seven **Council** Fires." Three **culture** groups make up the nation. They include the Lakota, Dakota, and Nakota. These are also the three **dialects** of the confederacy's shared language.

The confederacy's homeland spans across northern woodlands and the **Great Plains**. It includes many states in today's United States. It also includes four of today's Canadian **provinces**.

THE NAME *SIOUX*

Sioux was first used by the French. It means "little snakes." It is a mistranslation of an Ojibwe word. It has been used to negatively describe the People of the Seven Council Fires. Members of this confederacy may prefer to be recognized by their culture group or other more individual identifiers.

TRADITIONAL SIOUX LIFE

ILLUSTRATION OF A VILLAGE

TIPI

The People of the Seven Council Fires believe in the strength of **kinship**. Each nation relies on one another. They recognize the importance of relatives. Their **ancestors** lived in small groups called *tiospaye*. Members of a tiospaye shared a family line. Their homes, called tipis, were often organized into a circle.

The Lakota, Dakota, and Nakota also share kinship with animals. Like people, animals also make up nations. The bison nation and horse nation are especially important. Both became essential to the survival of the Lakota's ancestors.

ANIMAL NATIONS

Eagles hold special meaning for the Lakota, Dakota, and Nakota. They stand for bravery and courage.

LAKOTA BISON HIDE PAINTING

Lakota ancestors lived in the woodlands of today's Minnesota, Iowa, North Dakota, South Dakota, and Wisconsin. They moved to the northern Great Plains after facing conflicts with neighboring nations.

The Lakota became skilled bison hunters on the plains. By the mid-1700s, bison were their main source of food, shelter, and tools. The Lakota moved often to follow herds, especially in summer. Men hunted on horseback. Women dried and cooked meat. They also prepared hides for clothing and tipis. The Lakota used every part of the bison. It was shared amongst everyone in the community.

WHITE BISON

White bison are an important part of Lakota religion. The birth of a white bison calf means prayers will be answered and good things will come to the Lakota.

SIOUX RESOURCES

HIDE: BLANKETS, ROBES, TIPI COVERS

MEAT: FOOD

HORNS: BOWLS, CUPS

BISON

BONES: TOOLS

DUNG: FUEL FOR FIRES

STOMACH: CONTAINER FOR LIQUIDS

Dakota and Nakota ancestors once lived in areas of today's southern Alberta and Montana. Their land stretched into Ontario, Minnesota, North and South Dakota, and Wisconsin. The Nations often moved their villages with the seasons. They moved where they were able to best hunt and gather food. Men hunted deer, elk, bison, and other animals. Women farmed and gathered food. Wild rice was an important food.

WILD RICE

LAKE MILLE LACS, MINNESOTA, ORIGINAL LAND OF THE DAKOTA

NAKOTA CHIEF WALKING BUFFALO

Their ancestors made villages along rivers and lakes. They built large summer houses covered in bark. Winter homes were smaller. People who later moved to the western plains lived in tipis.

EUROPEAN CONTACT

UPPER DAKOTA SIOUX BANDS SIGNING THE TREATY OF TRAVERSE DES SIOUX, 1851

The People of the Seven Council Fires first met European traders in the 1600s. Their meetings were peaceful. But in the 1800s, Americans began moving onto the plains. The U.S. government forced the Nations to sign **treaties**. The government took most of their land. The Lakota, Dakota, and Nakota struggled to continue their **traditional** way of life.

The U.S. government **violated** the treaties. Conflicts began. Dakota and Lakota warriors fought against the U.S. in 1862. But they lost. Afterward, 38 Dakota people were **executed**. It became the largest single-day mass execution in U.S. history.

DAKOTA 38 MEMORIAL IN MANKATO, MINNESOTA

An 1868 treaty created the Great Sioux **Reservation**. It also provided hunting land. But U.S. government leaders began a program to kill the bison population throughout the 1800s. This greatly affected the Sioux's way of life. Meanwhile, conflict increased. Gold discoveries in the Black Hills led to the Great Sioux War in 1876.

The U.S. government took more land through the rest of the 1800s. It also forced children into government-run schools. The schools worked to remove the Sioux culture from the children. Challenges continued into the 1900s. But the Sioux survived through efforts to destroy them.

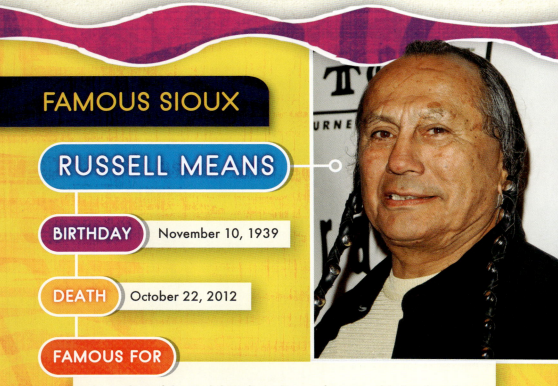

FAMOUS SIOUX

RUSSELL MEANS

BIRTHDAY — November 10, 1939

DEATH — October 22, 2012

FAMOUS FOR — A member of the Oglala Lakota Sioux who was a Native American rights activist known for protesting against the mistreatment of Native American people

LITTLE BIGHORN BATTLEFIELD NATIONAL MONUMENT

CRAZY HORSE AND SITTING BULL

Crazy Horse and Sitting Bull were Lakota leaders and warriors. They fought for their land and rights in the 1800s. They are best known for their efforts during the Great Sioux War and the Battle of the Little Bighorn.

LIFE TODAY

Today, over 100,000 people are the **descendants** of the People of the Seven Council Fires. Many people who live on reservations raise cattle. Some work in casinos owned by Sioux governments. Many descendants also live throughout the world. They work in business, health care, education, and many other fields.

The Lakota, Dakota, and Nakota are divided further into **bands**. Some bands have their own land. Others share land with other bands or nations. Many bands are located in North and South Dakota. Other reservations are in Minnesota, Montana, Nebraska, and Canada.

PINE RIDGE RESERVATION IN SOUTH DAKOTA

17

Each Lakota, Dakota, and Nakota band is an independent nation. They have their own governments. Tribal Councils create laws. Council members are elected. They work for the members of the band they represent. Bands also have tribal courts that help uphold the laws.

GOVERNMENT OF THE STANDING ROCK SIOUX TRIBE

TRIBAL COUNCIL
- Chairman
- Vice Chairman
- Secretary
- 14 council members

ROSEBUD SIOUX TRIBAL COUNCIL MEMBER WITH THE U.S. SECRETARY OF THE INTERIOR

Each government provides services. They create strong and healthy communities. Police help enforce laws and safety. Health and social services provide care to band members. Many bands also run businesses. These earn money for government services and provide jobs.

19

CONTINUING TRADITIONS

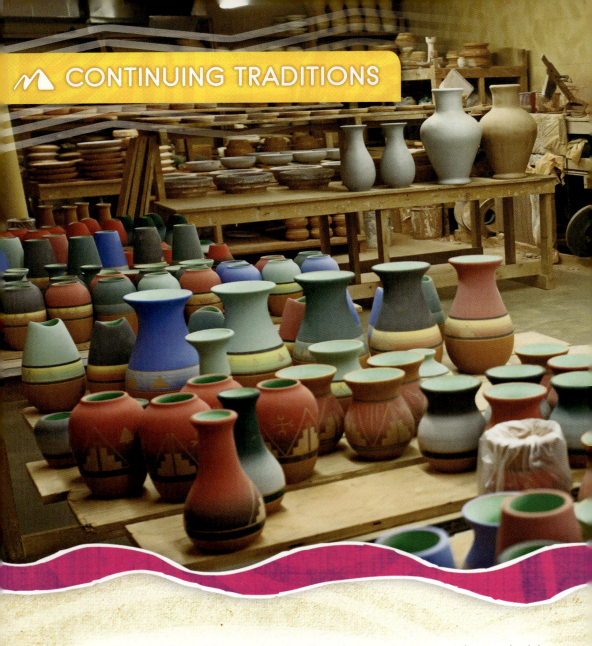

Each Sioux band has individual traditions. Many traditions hold the basic values that were practiced by their Lakota, Dakota, and Nakota ancestors. Like all cultures, people make changes to fit their own beliefs and ways of life. These changes have allowed the Lakota, Dakota, and Nakota to maintain their values.

ROSEBUD SIOUX ARTIST

BEAD AND QUILLWORK ART

Some Sioux artists use traditional practices to make their own unique creations. Sioux ancestors used paint, quills, and beads. These showed the beauty of everyday objects. Today, artists incorporate these materials to help maintain their culture.

21

CHEYENNE RIVER SIOUX TRIBE FAIR

Ceremonies are important religious practices. Many Lakota come together each year for the Sun Dance. This ceremony honors *Wakan Tanka*, or the Creator. People from many bands and nations come together for this ceremony.

Lakota, Dakota, and Nakota have *wacipis*, or **Pow Wows**, throughout the year. Songs and dancing are at the center of these gatherings. Singers and drummers often play traditional songs. The songs provide rhythm for dancers. Dancers often wear important clothing while participating in dance competitions. They dance in a circle to represent the circle of life.

LAKOTA MUSIC SYMBOLS

Lakota songs and dances carry history and help connect people to reality.

DRUM = THUNDER

RATTLE = RAIN

FLUTE = WIND

VOICE = LIGHTNING

FIGHT TODAY, BRIGHT TOMORROW

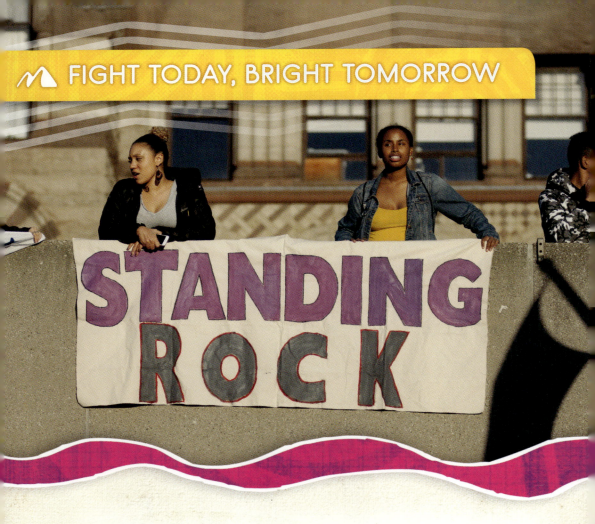

The U.S. government has continually violated the Fort Laramie Treaty of 1851. In 2017, the Dakota Access Pipeline began pumping oil from North Dakota to Illinois. One section passes close to the Standing Rock Sioux Reservation.

The Standing Rock Sioux have protested the pipeline. They state an oil spill would damage drinking water and cultural sites. They have fought for an **environmental** study to be more seriously considered. The courts agreed in early 2022. But in 2023, the public was still waiting for a review of the study. The pipeline continued to pump oil.

OIL BARRELS

In 2017, about 570,000 barrels of oil were pumped each day through the Dakota Access Pipeline. The amount was approved to increase to 1.1 million barrels per day in 2022.

Many Lakota, Dakota, and Nakota people work to keep their **heritage**. The Stoney Nakoda First Nation in Canada recently created a textbook to teach the Stoney Nakoda language. In 2019, the Shakopee Mdewakanton Sioux Community formed Understand Native Minnesota. This program aims to provide accurate and respectful education about Native Americans in schools.

UNDERSTAND NATIVE MINNESOTA WEBSITE

SHAKOPEE MDEWAKANTON SIOUX COMMUNITY RESERVATION

WOUNDED KNEE MASSACRE MONUMENT

In 2022, the Oglala Sioux and Cheyenne River Sioux bought land around the 1890 Wounded Knee Massacre site. This purchase allows them to keep this land safe. The People of the Seven Council Fires have stayed strong throughout history. They will thrive into the future!

TIMELINE

1862
In Mankato, Minnesota, 38 Dakota men are executed as a result of the Dakota War

MID-1600s
Groups within the People of the Seven Council Fires begin moving westward and southward from their original lands

1851
The Fort Laramie Treaty of 1851 is signed, defining territories the Sioux are expected to stay on

1862
Americans begin traveling through Sioux territory to reach Montana goldfields, violating the Fort Laramie Treaty of 1851, leading to Red Cloud's War from 1866 to 1868

MID-1700s
The Lakota adapt to horse culture

1876
Sioux Chief Sitting Bull's forces defeat Colonel George A. Custer and his troops in the Battle of the Little Bighorn

1980
The U.S. Supreme Court awards the Sioux over $100 million for taking the Black Hills in 1877, but the Sioux turn down the reward and continue to fight to get their land back

1890
U.S. Army troops open fire on a group of around 300 Lakota men, women, and children resulting in the Wounded Knee Massacre

1868
The Fort Laramie Treaty of 1868 is signed, forcing the Sioux to give up more land and establishing the Great Sioux Reservation

2016
The Standing Rock Sioux, other Native American Nations, and their supporters begin protesting the building of the Dakota Access Pipeline

GLOSSARY

ancestors—relatives who lived long ago

bands—groups of people who live as communities and share a culture

ceremonies—sets of actions performed in a particular way, often as part of religious worship

confederacy—a group of Native American nations

council—a group of people who meet to run a government

culture—the beliefs, arts, and ways of life in a place or society

descendants—people related to a person or group of people who lived at an earlier time

dialects—ways of speaking particular languages

environmental—related to the natural surroundings of an area

executed—put to death

Great Plains—a region of flat or gently rolling land in the central United States and parts of southern Canada

heritage—the traditions, achievements, and beliefs that are part of the history of a group of people

kinship—a relationship among people

Pow Wows—Native American gatherings that usually include dancing

provinces—large areas of a country that have their own governments

reservation—land set aside by the U.S. government for the forced removal of a Native American community from their original land

traditional—related to customs, ideas, or beliefs handed down from one generation to the next

treaties—official agreements between two groups

violated—broke or failed to keep promises

TO LEARN MORE

AT THE LIBRARY

MacCarald, Clara. *The Standing Rock Sioux Challenge the Dakota Access Pipeline.* Lake Elmo, Minn.: Focus Readers, 2019.

Marcks, Betty. *The Blackfeet.* Minneapolis, Minn.: Bellwether Media, 2024.

Rathburn, Betsy. *South Dakota.* Minneapolis, Minn.: Bellwether Media, 2022.

ON THE WEB

FACTSURFER

Factsurfer.com gives you a safe, fun way to find more information.

1. Go to www.factsurfer.com.

2. Enter "the Sioux" into the search box and click 🔍.

3. Select your book cover to see a list of related content.

INDEX

animal nations, 6, 7
bands, 12, 16, 17, 18, 19, 20, 21, 22, 24, 26, 27
bison, 6, 8, 9, 10, 14
confederacy, 4
Crazy Horse, 15
culture, 4, 14, 20, 21, 24
Dakota, 4, 6, 7, 10, 11, 12, 13, 16, 18, 20, 23, 24, 26
Dakota Access Pipeline, 24, 25
future, 27
government of the Standing Rock Sioux Tribe, 18
Great Plains, 4, 5, 8, 11, 12
Great Sioux War, 14, 15
heritage, 26
history, 6, 8, 10, 11, 12, 13, 14, 15, 21, 24, 25, 26, 27
homeland, 4, 5, 8, 10, 12, 14, 15, 16, 17
kinship, 6
Lakota, 4, 6, 7, 8, 9, 12, 13, 15, 16, 17, 18, 19, 20, 21, 22, 23, 24, 26, 27
Lakota music symbols, 23

language, 4, 26
map, 5, 16
Means, Russell, 14
members, 4, 6, 18, 19
Nakota, 4, 6, 7, 10, 11, 12, 16, 18, 20, 23, 26
name, 4
Pow Wows, 23
religion, 9, 22
reservations, 14, 16, 17, 24, 26
Sioux resources, 9
Sitting Bull, 15
Sun Dance, 22
timeline, 28–29
traditions, 8, 9, 10, 11, 12, 20, 21, 22, 23
treaties, 12, 13, 14, 24
tribal governments, 16, 18, 19
Understand Native Minnesota, 26
U.S. government, 12, 13, 14, 19, 24
Wounded Knee Massacre, 27

The images in this book are reproduced through the courtesy of: Hemis/ Alamy, front cover; Hiart/ Wikipedia, p. 3; turtix, pp. 4-5; Alan King engraving/ Alamy, p. 6; Colin Edwards Wildside, p. 7 (eagle); Nancy G Western Photography, Nancy Greifenhagen/ Alamy, p. 7 (horses); ClassicStock/ Alamy, p. 8 (preparing a hide); World History Archive/ Alamy, p. 8 (hide painting); Ken Gillespie Photography/ Alamy, p. 9 (white bison); VladGans, pp. 9 (bison), 31; John_Brueske, p. 10; Dionisvera, p. 10 (wild rice); Vintage collection 216/ Alamy, p. 11; Minnesota Historical Society/ Wikipedia, p. 12; Trevor Cokley/ AP Images, p. 13; s_bukley, p. 14; Carol Barrington/ Alamy, p. 15; Stania Kasula/ Alamy, pp. 16-17; Jim West/ Alamy, pp. 17, 20-21; unknown/ Wikipedia, p. 18; Matthew Brown/ AP Images, p. 19; Shiiko Alexander/ Alamy, p. 21; Cecilia Colussi Stock/ Alamy, p. 22; Barbara Ash/ Alamy, p. 23 (drum); Album/ Alamy, p. 23 (rattle); unknown/ Library of Congress, p. 23 (flute); MasPix/ Alamy, p. 23 (voice); Arindam Banerjee, p. 24; Puwadol Jaturawutthichai, p. 25 (oil barrels); Diego G Diaz, p. 25; Prathankarnpap, p. 26 (Understand Native Minnesota); Jacob Boomsma/ Getty Images, p. 26; BC Images, p. 27; Science History Images/ Alamy, p. 28 (mid-1700s); David F. Barry/ Wikipedia, p. 29 (1876); northlight, p. 29 (2016).